McCall Collection of Modern Art

Modigliani and the Painters of Montparnasse

by HELEN I. HUBBARD

Published by Fratelli Fabbri Editori,
Publishers, Milan, Italy, and

The McCall Publishing Company
New York, New York

The Years of Study in Italy and in Montmartre

In the early years of the twentieth century, Paris was the undisputed capital of the Western art world. Young artists flocked there from every part of Europe and from as far away as the Orient. Several of the most talented were of Jewish extraction, from the ghettos of Middle and Eastern Europe. They came to participate in the intellectual and artistic ferment that was taking place in Paris, to meet and mingle with other artists, writers, and critics, and to enjoy the freedom, actual as well as artistic, of the Bohemian life.

The frequently used term "School of Paris" is vague and inconclusive; it identifies artists, foreign as well as French, who worked in Paris from the end of the nineteenth century through the first half of the twentieth. But the term is also, and more profitably, employed in a more limited way to designate only those artists, foreign for the most part, who lived and worked in Paris but who remained aloof from the great central art movements, Cubism, Abstractionism, and Surrealism, which were then developing.

These artists had very little in common. They did not have similar artistic beliefs nor did they work in the same style. They were artists of stature, but not great innovators. They were traditionalists rather than revolutionaries. This does not mean that they lacked originality or individuality. Each developed an intensely personal artistic style. But the artistic "language" that they used was a traditional one, not one of the new and difficult languages being invented and developed by Picasso, Braque, Matisse, and their followers.

Montmartre and Montparnasse

Lacking any unifying characteristic beyond their traditionalism, they are principally tied together by geography and the fact that they lived and worked in Paris for most of their lives. More precisely, they lived and worked in Montmartre, "the Butte," on the Right Bank of the Seine, and Montparnasse, the Latin Quarter, on the Left Bank. Together these two quarters constituted Bohemia, the artistic heart of the city. Indeed the School of Paris might well have been called the School of Montmartre and Montparnasse.

Unquestionably the prince of this Bohemia was Amedeo Modigliani (Mo-dēl-'yän-ē). Of Italian parentage, he came from Leghorn on the Ligurian coast of Italy. His family had once been of some importance, an ancestral branch of it having given its name to the village of Modigliani south of Rome. But the family wealth and prestige had dissipated, and Modigliani was brought up in very modest circumstances.

As a boy his health was delicate. A particularly serious pulmonary attack was followed by a long period of convalescence, during which his mother provided him with drawing materials as a means of entertaining him. Further attacks occurred during his adolescence, but in spite of them he managed to study at art schools in Rome, Florence, and Venice. But his destination was Paris. His doting mother scraped together whatever financial aid she could, and finally, in late 1905 or early 1906, he arrived in Montmartre.

Fifty years earlier Montmartre had been merely a pretty village located on a hilltop on the outskirts of Paris. It was a half-farm, half-suburban community of picturesque windmills and steep, narrow streets winding between houses with whitewashed walls and shuttered windows and doorways draped with tangles of morning glory. But its character gradually changed. Over the years, as the city surrounded it, Montmartre became a place of recreation and amusement, a locale for open-air restaurants, for cafes and dance halls. Artists discovered Montmartre. The Impressionists enjoyed its pleasures, still relatively harmless, and depicted them on canvas. Its windmills gave their names to such artistically famous places as the Moulin de la Galette and the Moulin Rouge. Gradually its metamorphosis took on a more sinister aspect, as portrayed by Toulouse-Lautrec. Its charm grew more potent and more poisonous. It became the residence of pimps and prostitutes, drunks and drug addicts, waiters and restaurateurs, and entertainers, as well as artists, poets, writers, and musicians.

Montparnasse was undergoing a similar change. It had been a sprawling community of artisans and shopkeepers and students before artists adopted it as a place where they could live cheaply. Its cafes, such as Le Dôme and La Rotonde, became the meeting places for creative individuals of all types. *La vie de Bohème,* the Bohemian life, held sway. Into this life Modigliani plunged like an arrow finding its mark.

He had been a beautiful child, and, at the age of twenty-one, when he arrived in Paris, he was an incredibly handsome young man. He was slight of build, his features flawless, his eyes darkly passionate. And he had an innate elegance and aristocracy of manner that led a friend, the sculptor Zadkine, to describe him as "a young god masquerading as a workman in his Sunday best." His Sunday best he wore everyday, as it constituted his entire wardrobe. It was a corduroy suit, with which he wore a checked shirt and a red belt.

His face, his bearing, and his manner were so appealing that during his first years in Paris he attracted more attention as a man than as an artist. Yet he seemed unaware of his charm and was almost childishly eager to please.

"I knew him well," Vlaminck said. "I knew him when he was hungry. I have seen him drunk. But in no instance did I ever find him lacking in nobility or generosity. I never knew him to be guilty of the least baseness, although I have seen him irascible at having to admit the power of money, which he scorned but which could so hamper him and hurt his pride."

He was a poet and an impassioned lover of Dante; he could recite, drunk or sober, in Italian, whole cantos of the *Divine Comedy,* to which his friends were constrained to listen whether they understood or not.

Modigliani's life in Montmartre, and later in Montparnasse on the opposite bank of the Seine, epitomizes in every detail the popular notion of the Bohemian life. It has been called "a long-drawn suicide." A zeal for self-destruction was inherent in his nature. Talented and tormented, tempestuous, overwrought, he was foreordained to destroy himself with an energy that seemed, in some strange way, to be an inversion, like a photographic negative, of the creative energy that formed his art. Creation and destruction appeared with him to be simultaneous manifestations of the same force.

Perhaps, too, his urge for self-destruction was an endemic Italian disease. His boyhood in Italy had been profoundly influenced by a "lost generation" of Italian writers whose works were one long, unmitigated cry of rage and despair. Their intolerance of life had left a permanent scar on him. He rarely smiled. In one of his poems he speaks of "the great soundless tumult in the midnight of the soul." The phrase is heavy with adolescent emotionalism, but it is not an exaggeration. There was little sun in his soul, and even less peace.

The weapons he used to commit his fourteen-year-long suicide were alcohol and little pellets of hashish. Both were readily available in Montmartre and Montparnasse for very little money. When he had no money at all, which was often, he would sit in a bar and make pencil portraits of customers in exchange for a drink. Vlaminck in his memoirs describes Modigliani sketching at La Rotonde: "With a lordly gesture, like some millionaire distributing largesse, he would hand out his drawings, as if he were paying with a large bank note for the glass of whiskey to which he had just been treated."

The artist Fournier gives us another description of such a scene. "Modigliani would sit down at a small table, open his sketchbook and caress the page with his hand. Then he would stare fixedly into the eyes of his model, as if hypnotizing him. His pencil would begin to run in all directions over his paper, and he would seem to relax, humming. Suddenly he would stop, stroke the paper with his hand, and furiously correct some little detail. If his first sketch failed to satisfy him, he would assume an air of disenchantment and indifference before violently attacking a new sheet. Finally he would offer his drawing to the model in exchange for a drink. Then he would disappear."

Alcohol was not all that Modigliani bought with his sketches. When he dined at "Chez Rosalie," he often paid for his meal with a drawing. Since Rosalie had no use for art, she put the drawings in the cellar, where the rats ate them. According to Zadkine, who occasionally dined with Modigliani at Rosalie's, "the rats would sometimes sneak up into the tiny kitchen with bits of the drawings still hanging from their mouths."

Modigliani did little painting during his first eight or nine years in Paris. He produced many drawings—drawing was as necessary to him as breathing—and some sculpture. In spite of the fact that sculpture was his principal interest during these years, very little of it has survived. He disposed of much of it in his destructive rages, and much was abandoned in his frequent moves about Montparnasse, due to unpaid rent. His experience with sculpture is evident in the two drawings of caryatids (Plates 4 and 5), which helped him to develop his ultimate painting style. Probably the principal reason why he abandoned sculpture in favor of painting after about 1914 was his absolute poverty. Stone and marble cost far more than canvas.

One of the few paintings Modigliani did during his early years is *Study for "The Cello Player"* (Plate 2). The chief influence apparent here is that of Cézanne. The palette is entirely Cézanne's, with its blue-greens and siennas. The distortion of the figure and the color modeling, especially in the face, are Cézanne's too. There is an emotional quality, however, that is not to be found in Cézanne's portraits. *"The Cello Player"* is actually quite Expressionist in feeling. In style it is still derivative. Modigliani has not yet achieved the individuality of style that would later set his work so clearly apart from that of any other artist.

In 1914 two events occurred that were important to him as a man and even more important to him as an artist. He was introduced to two people, both poets who appear to have written very little poetry. The first, Beatrice Hastings, was an Englishwoman; the second, Léopold Zborowski, was Polish.

Beatrice Hastings lived with Modigliani for several years. Although she was a cold woman and her attachment to him seems not to have been profound, her influence on him was good. His production had slackened to the merest trickle. Something in his relationship with Beatrice Hastings acted as a catalyst in his career. He suddenly stirred from his artistic dead center and began to paint. "Paint, my dear boy," she is reported to have said to him. "After all, you're a painter, aren't you?" And paint he did. His career really began with Beatrice Hastings. From 1914 until his death in 1920, he painted continually.

Léopold Zborowski

The Pole, Léopold Zborowski, became one of Modigliani's most devoted friends. Zborowski soon abandoned his study of literature and became an art dealer. He did this partly in the hope of making a decent living for himself and his wife, but principally because of his love of art and his sincere desire to help impoverished and talented artists. His efforts on behalf of his artist friends, particularly Soutine and Modigliani, were unceasing and self-sacrificing.

The Paintings of Modigliani

Modigliani's art is concerned exclusively with the human face and figure. Together his portraits constitute the face of his world and his time, the last real Bohemia. He painted no elegant social portraits, but musicians, sculptors, artists, dealers, servants, tradespeople, apprentices, models, mistresses, his

4

friends and their wives. His work includes no landscapes or still lifes. Even the backgrounds of his paintings are reduced to a few simple planes or color divisions. He makes no use of interior "settings" to convey intimations of character or social class, as portraitists often do. Nor does he enjoy painting elaborate costumes, as Renoir, Degas, and Lautrec did. His models are clad in the simplest of apparel. Modigliani's interest was not in externals.

In spite of the fact that Modigliani developed a style so personal that one recognizes his paintings fairly easily, he nevertheless expresses the personality of each model. Paradoxically one discovers, by comparing early portraits with later ones of the same person, that the more he developed his own individuality of style, the more he was able to express the individuality of his model. At a casual viewing, his passionate adherence to this style may appear to be monotonous: the elongated necks, small heads, simplified forms, distorted features, eyes like small, oval seeds. But closer study reveals great variety and subtlety within this framework.

Soutine

Compare, for instance, the portraits of two men, his intimate artist friend, Chaïm Soutine, and the dealer, Paul Guillaume. Soutine was a robust and virile Lithuanian, ten years younger than Modigliani, to whom Soutine once said, "If I weren't certain of making a fortune out of my painting, I'd drop it immediately and go in for boxing." In Modigliani's portrait of him (Plate 10), we are made to feel his naïve enthusiasm, his intensity, sensuality, and peasant strength. Furthermore, by using the rich, strong colors that Soutine favored, and by applying them in his manner, in a thick impasto, Modigliani also gives an impression of Soutine's own painting style.

Guillaume

The portrait of Guillaume, on the other hand (Plate 12), is painted in a different color scheme and in a completely different manner. Instead of the feeling of sturdiness and strength in the Soutine portrait, we have the impression of an overcivilized, rather supercilious character, selfish and conceited. The slope of the shoulders, the tilt of the head, the angle of the hat, and the position of the gloved hand—all combine to create this impression. Modigliani may have been offended by Guillaume's comment on his work, "There's nothing French about it, and that's a great pity, because the young man has a real gift."

The Nude Portraits

The most ambitious of Modigliani's paintings are his nudes. They are erotic figures, unequivocally nude—they have been called "the nudest of nudes." They look very real and very physical, not like goddesses but like adult women (Plates 22 and 23). For Modigliani's first one-man show, four of these nudes were placed in the window. Considered indecent, they were quickly removed by order of the police as "an intolerable offense to public morals."

But Modigliani's sensuality was blended with idealism. While these figures appear real, they are actually distorted and elongated into an elegance of form that is not real at all. They present the contradiction of "idealized sensuality."

On a trip to the south of France, arranged and paid for by Zborowski, who was worried about his friend's health, Modigliani called to pay his respects to the aging Renoir. "Paint with joy, young man," Renoir said. "Paint with the same joy you feel when making love to a woman. You must caress your canvases, caress them for a long time. I spend days and days stroking the backsides of my nudes before I finish them." Modigliani's sensuality was not equal to the occasion. Distaste overcame him. He managed to stammer, "I, Monsieur, do not like backsides," and fled from the room.

All of Modigliani's paintings, nudes and portraits alike, are distinguished chiefly by their linear quality. This line is marvelously graceful and decorative, and at the same time it expresses deep space. It is not mere outline or contour but surrounds and models the forms and indicates the space around them.

Like Picasso and Matisse, Modigliani was a superb draftsman, and also like Picasso, he drew in a single, continuous line, without lifting the pencil from the paper. His virtuosity in drawing made it possible for him to catch a likeness in very few strokes, and his economy of line contributes to the power of his portraits. Often he gives, with his concise line, not only a penetrating character study but also his own feeling about the model. For instance we sense from his portraits of them that he was fond of Soutine and disenchanted with Guillaume. And, as we look at his portrait of Jeanne Hébuterne (Plate 26), we understand instantly that he was desperately in love with her.

He met Jeanne Hébuterne in 1917, and their love seems to have been immediate and mutual. She was an art student, a simple, shy, religious girl, whose classmates called her "Noix de coco" or "Coconut." She wore the plainest of clothes, flat-heeled shoes, and no makeup. She was not pretty in a conventional way, but her face had a haunting, spiritual quality that Modigliani conveys in this portrait. What he chiefly expresses here, however, is his love. It shows in the gentleness of the curves, the pale delicacy of the skin, the softness of the modeling, the unswerving eyes. There is love in the luminous blue glow that sets off the beauty of the chestnut hair. In the words that Modigliani's idol, Dante, used to describe his Beatrice, this portrait represents "her image, that was with me always, with an exultation of love to subdue me."

Modigliani painted twenty portraits of Jeanne in the three years that they had together. In 1920, exhausted by poverty, illness, drugs, and alcohol, he was hospitalized. "I am leaving the mud behind. I now know all there is to know, and soon I'll be no more than a handful of dust," he said to Zborowski. "I've kissed my wife. Please take her back to her parents. This is the right moment. Anyhow we're sure of eternal happiness, she and I, whatever happens.''

Modigliani died a few days later, followed within another day by Jeanne. On the physical plane his life had been a sorry one. Of the goods of this world he had had almost nothing. But he had never felt spiritually poor. On the contrary he looked upon himself and his fellow artists as different and above the world at large. On the margin of one of his drawings he had written, ''Life is a gift from the few to the many, from those who know and have to those who do not know and have not.'' There is a suggestion of youthful arrogance in this phrase that one gladly overlooks in contrasting the pain and suffering, the cold and hunger of Modigliani as a ''have not'' in an indifferent world with his gift as a ''have'' to that same world.

Contemporaries of Modigliani

It is interesting to compare Modigliani's work with that of his friends and contemporaries of the School of Paris. This can be readily done, as several artists frequently painted the same subject. Kisling's *Nude on a Red Couch* (Plate 51) and Foujita's *Youki, Goddess of the Snow* (Plate 56) may be compared with any of Modigliani's reclining nudes, and most viewers would acknowledge the vast superiority of Modigliani's work. Kisling's color is as harsh as Foujita's is dull. The clear outlines of both nudes, instead of modeling the forms and giving them solidity, as Modigliani's line does, make them look like shapes cut from cardboard. The compositions are either cluttered with too many forms and textures, as in the Kisling, or uninteresting and flat, as with Foujita.

Kisling was capable of very sharply characterized portraiture, however. *Jean Cocteau in His Studio* (Plate 50) admirably conveys the poet's personality.

André Derain and Modigliani both painted portraits of Zborowski (Plate 49 and 32). While the portraits may be equally valid as likenesses, Derain's is almost academic. It has no distinction stylistically. Modigliani's is a fine example of his mature and highly individual style — free-flowing, curved line, simplified and elongated forms, muted color harmonies, and concise but convincing expression of the subject's personality.

Chaïm Soutine was an artist quite as individual as Modigliani. They were very different, both as men and as artists. Soutine was homely, uncouth, uncultured, and his uncleanliness became the joke and legend of Montparnasse. Modigliani was handsome, courteous, highly cultured, and as fastidious as his poverty permitted. Modigliani's art was linear, based on virtuoso drawing, and it was permeated with a quiet melancholy. Soutine made no use of drawing, even as a preliminary step in his painting, but painted directly on the canvas.

Soutine was born in a rural ghetto in Lithuania, on the outskirts of Russia, the tenth of eleven children. His father was not a tailor, as is often said, but a mender of clothes, and his family was at the bottom level of village life. In such an environment it is astounding that he should have felt the desire to become an artist. He could not possibly have had any experience with art in his village. It was not only beyond his village experience but also outside his family and village tradition of Orthodox Judaism. Yet even as a young child his great urge was to draw, and he drew on any available surface. At the age of thirteen he ran away from home to avoid apprenticeship as a cobbler.

Eventually he found his way to Paris to become, with Modigliani and Pascin, one of the "peintres maudits," the "accursed painters," whose tormented natures, like an evil spell, were quite as responsible for their tragic lives as were external circumstances.

In contrast to the silence and reserve of Modigliani's portraits, which are felt more in *The Flower Vendor* (Plate 18) and *Gypsy Woman with Baby* (Plate 30) than in the Kisling portrait, Soutine's are noisy with color and movement. He prefers brilliant, almost visceral colors to Modigliani's more subtle tones. In fact, one critic uses the term "rotten with color" to describe Soutine's paintings. Soutine's studio was located in a swarming ghetto in Montmartre, next to a slaughterhouse, and several times he painted great carcasses of beef. It is quite possible that Soutine's color derives in part from the beautiful and brilliant colors of decomposition, which we find revolting only through association.

Perhaps the most extraordinary portrait Soutine ever did is *Woman in Red* (Plate 53). The distorted and richly colored forms seem to flow together. The features and fingers are like putty or partially melted wax. But the character study is unforgettable. And in spite of an apparently merciless exaggeration, carried to the point of grotesqueness, we feel Soutine's compassion. The ravaged face under its running makeup, the gallant smile, the flirtatious, antiquated costume and enormous picture hat—all are deeply moving.

Another individual but less virile talent was that of Jules Pascin, a Spanish-Italian artist from Bulgaria. His paintings are nervous, sensitive, delicate, animated. In subject matter they are very limited, depicting almost exclusively nude and seminude prostitutes and adolescents, as *Ginette and Mireille* (Plate 58), *The Blue Chemise* (Plate 59), and *Nude with Red Sandals* (Plate 60). His models are presented without indication of any emotion on the part of the artist other than a vague and melancholy sympathy. They are given no character or personality as individuals. Perhaps it is the soft, shimmering sameness of them that is disturbing; it hints at a dreaming, faceless degeneracy.

Today Montmartre and Montparnasse have changed very little. "And even if the furriers, wardrobe dealers, fortune-tellers, carriage builders, and dentists occupy the cafes today instead of Apollinaire, Picasso, Kisling, Modigliani, Derain, and Vlaminck, a light breeze still goes chasing around the kiosks and between the park benches, beckoning to the ghosts, summoning up the past."

PLATES

Tradition and Modernity of Figures: Amedeo Modigliani

PLATE 1   AMEDEO MODIGLIANI *Self-Portrait,* 1919 (100 x 65 cm) São Paulo, Sr. and
Sra. Francisco Matarazzo Sobrinho Collection (Photo: Mercurio)

PLATE 2   AMEDEO MODIGLIANI *Study for "The Cello Player,"* 1909 (73 x 60 cm) Paris, Dr. Paul Alexandre Collection

PLATE 3   AMEDEO MODIGLIANI *Reverie: Portrait of Frank Burty Haviland, c.* 1914 (61 x 50 cm) Los Angeles, County Museum, Mr. and Mrs. William Preston Harrison Collection (Photo: Giraudon)

13

PLATE 4   AMEDEO MODIGLIANI *Caryatid,* 1910–16 (53 x 43.6 cm) Paris, Musée National d'Art Moderne

PLATE 5   Amedeo Modigliani *Caryatid,* 1913–14 (90 x 70 cm) Milan, Private Collection

PLATE 6   AMEDEO MODIGLIANI *Henri Laurens Seated, c.* 1915 (81 x 60 cm) New Orleans, Mr. and Mrs. Robert J. Newman Collection

PLATE 7   AMEDEO MODIGLIANI *Antonio, c.* 1915 (80.5 x 45.5 cm) Paris, Louvre

PLATE 8   AMEDEO MODIGLIANI *Bride and Groom,* 1915–16 (55.2 x 46.3 cm) New York, Museum of Modern Art
(Gift of Frederic Clay Bartlett)

PLATE 9   AMEDEO MODIGLIANI *Madam Pompadour*, 1915 (61 x 50.4 cm) Chicago, Art Institute
of Chicago, Joseph Winterbotham Collection

19

PLATE 10   AMEDEO MODIGLIANI *Chaïm Soutine*, 1915 (38 x 28 cm) Stuttgart, Staatsgalerie

20

PLATE 11   AMEDEO MODIGLIANI *Moïse Kisling,* 1915 (37 x 29 cm) Milan, Private Collection

PLATE 12   AMEDEO MODIGLIANI *Portrait of Paul Guillaume*, 1915 (100 x 75 cm) Paris, Louvre

PLATE 13   AMEDEO MODIGLIANI *Beatrice Hastings,* 1915 (69 x 49 cm) Milan, Private Collection

PLATE 14   Amedeo Modigliani *The Servant Girl*, 1916 (73 x 54 cm) Zurich, Kunsthaus

PLATE 15   AMEDEO MODIGLIANI *La Jolie Epicière,* 1918 (100 x 65 cm) Paris, Private Collection
(Photo: Giraudon)

PLATE 16   AMEDEO MODIGLIANI *Woman with a Black Necktie,* 1917 (65 x 50 cm) Paris, Private Collection

PLATE 17   AMEDEO MODIGLIANI *Jacques Lipchitz and His Wife,* 1916 (80 x 53 cm) Chicago, Art Institute of Chicago, Helen Birch Bartlett Memorial Collection

PLATE 18   AMEDEO MODIGLIANI *The Flower Vendor*, 1917 (116.5 x 72 cm) New York,
Florence M. Schoenborn Collection (Photo: Pollitzer)

PLATE 19   AMEDEO MODIGLIANI *Redheaded Woman with Pendant Necklace,* 1917 (92 x 60 cm) Brussels,
H. Belien Collection

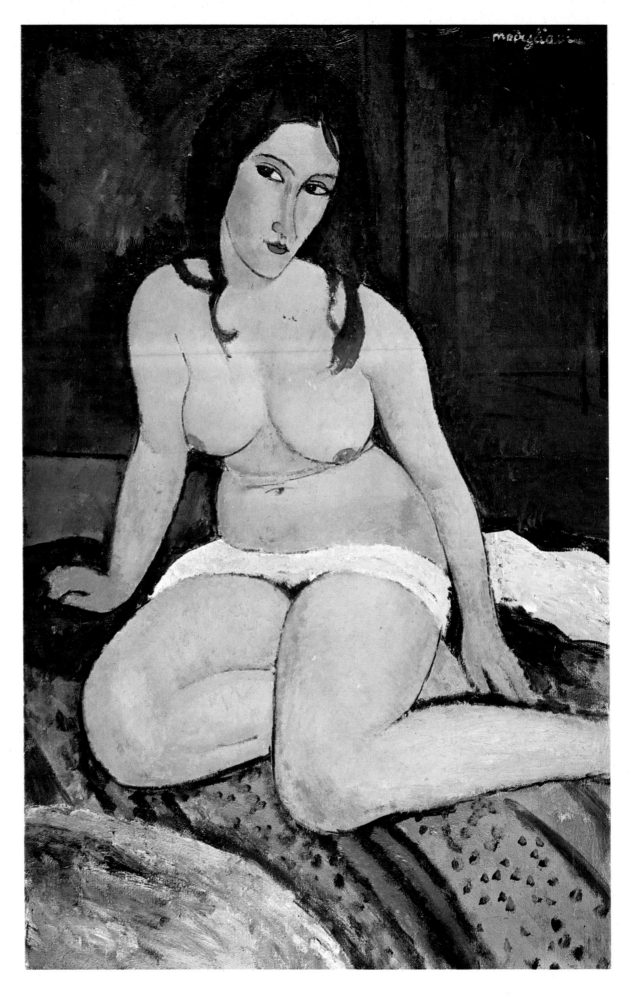

PLATE 20   AMEDEO MODIGLIANI *Seated Nude,* 1917 (116 x 73 cm) Antwerp, Koninklijk Museum
voor Schone Kunsten

PLATE 21   AMEDEO MODIGLIANI *Reclining Nude*, 1917–18 (60 x 92 cm) Milan, Private Collection

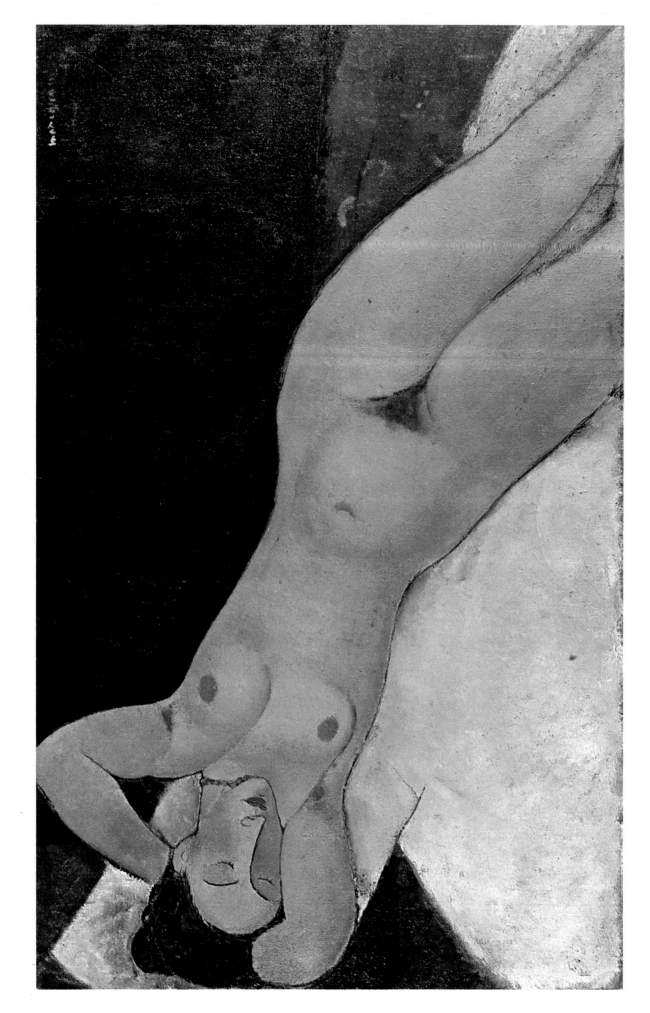

PLATE 22   AMEDEO MODIGLIANI *Reclining Nude with Necklace*, 1917 (73 x 116 cm) New York, Solomon R. G-ggenheim Museum

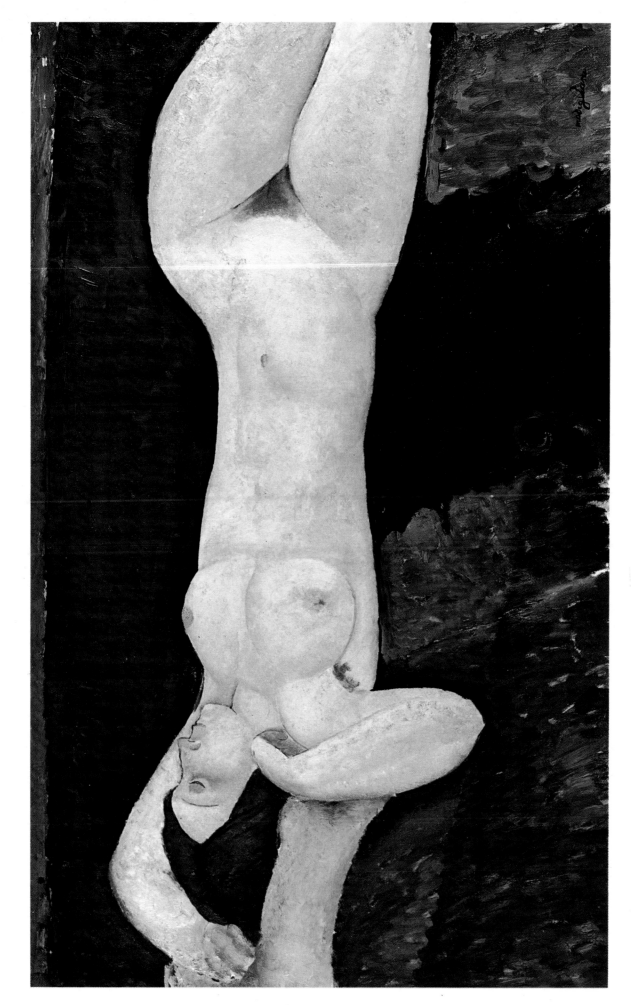

PLATE 23   AMEDEO MODIGLIANI *Reclining Nude* (Le Grand Nu), *c.* 1919 (73 x 116 cm) New York, Museum of Modern Art, Mrs. Simon Guggenheim Fund

PLATE 24   AMEDEO MODIGLIANI *Man Leaning on a Table,* 1918 (93 x 55 cm) Milan,
Private Collection

PLATE 25   AMEDEO MODIGLIANI *Léopold Survage,* 1918 (61.5 x 46 cm) Helsinki, Kunstmuseum Athenäum

35

PLATE 26   AMEDEO MODIGLIANI *Jeanne Hébuterne,* 1919 (46 x 29 cm) Switzerland,
Private Collection (Photo: Mercurio)

PLATE 27   AMEDEO MODIGLIANI *Lunia Czechowska*, 1918 (46 x 38 cm) Paris, Private Collection

PLATE 28   AMEDEO MODIGLIANI *Jeanne Hébuterne Seated in a Chair*, 1918–19 (100 x 65 cm)
Los Angeles, Mr. and Mrs. Norton Simon Collection

PLATE 29   AMEDEO MODIGLIANI *The Young Apprentice*, 1918 (100 x 65 cm) Paris, Louvre

PLATE 30   AMEDEO MODIGLIANI *Gypsy Woman with Baby*, 1919 (116 x 73 cm)
Washington, D. C., National Gallery of Art, Chester Dale Collection

PLATE 31   AMEDEO MODIGLIANI *Lunia Czechowska: Woman with White Collar,* 1916 (92 x 60 cm) Grenoble,
Musée de Peinture et de Sculpture

PLATE 32   AMEDEO MODIGLIANI *Léopold Zborowski*, 1917 (107 x 66 cm) São Paulo, Museo de Arte

PLATE 33   AMEDEO MODIGLIANI *Almaïsa,* 1917 (92 x 54 cm) Switzerland, Private Collection

PLATE 34   AMEDEO MODIGLIANI *Nude, c.* 1917 (92 x 60 cm) London, Courtauld Institute Galleries

PLATE 35   AMEDEO MODIGLIANI *Margherita,* 1916 (81 x 40 cm) Domodossola, Private Collection

45

PLATE 36   AMEDEO MODIGLIANI *Hanka Zborowski Seated with Hands Clasped,* 1919 (100 x 65 cm) Paris,
Private Collection (Photo: Giraudon)

PLATE 37   AMEDEO MODIGLIANI *Lunia Czechowska with a Fan*, 1919 (100 x 65 cm) Paris, Musée National d'Art Moderne

PLATE 38   AMEDEO MODIGLIANI *The Yellow Sweater: Jeanne Hébuterne*, 1919 (100 x 65 cm)
New York, Solomon R. Guggenheim Museum

PLATE 39   AMEDEO MODIGLIANI *Boy in a Blue Jacket,* 1918 (92 x 61.5 cm) New York,
Solomon R. Guggenheim Museum

49

PLATE 40   AMEDEO MODIGLIANI *Monsieur Mario,* 1919 (116 x 73 cm) Zurich, Franz Meyer
Collection

Other Artists of Montparnasse

PLATE 41   KEES VAN DONGEN *The Finger on the Cheek,* 1910 (65 x 54 cm) Rotterdam, Boymans van Beuningen Museum

PLATE 42 KEES VAN DONGEN *The Two Cousins,* 1906 (100 x 81 cm) Paris, Odermatt Collection

PLATE 43   KEES VAN DONGEN *La Belle Fernande,* 1905 (100 x 81 cm) Paris, Private Collection (Photo: Mercurio)

PLATE 44   MAURICE VLAMINCK *Le père Bouju,* 1900 (74 x 49 cm) Paris, Private Collection
(Photo: Giraudon)

PLATE 45   MAURICE VLAMINCK *The Dancer of the Cafe "Rat Mort,"* 1906 (73 x 64 cm) Paris, Private Collection
(Photo: Mercurio)

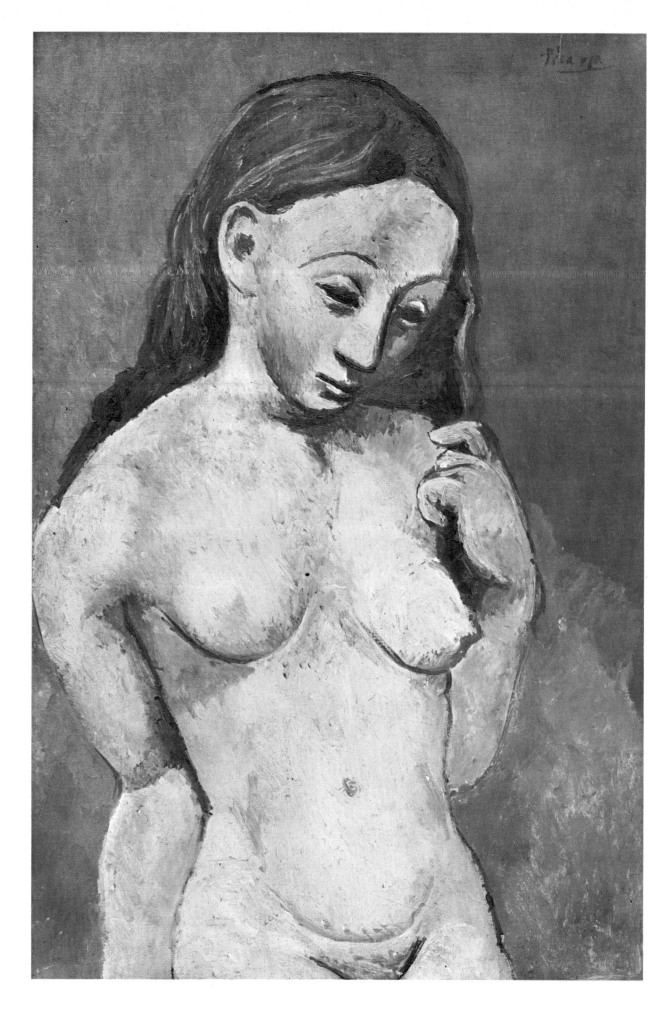

PLATE 46   PABLO PICASSO *Nude on a Red Background,* 1906 (81 x 54 cm) Paris, Louvre

PLATE 47   ANDRÉ DERAIN *Paul Poiret*, 1915 (101 x 73 cm) Grenoble, Musée de Peinture et de Sculpture

PLATE 48   ANDRÉ DERAIN *Mme Paul Guillaume with a Big Hat*, 1929 (91 x 73 cm) Paris, Louvre

PLATE 53   Chaïm Soutine *Woman in Red,* 1922 (63.5 x 53 cm) New York, Dr. and Mrs. Harry
Bakwin Collection

PLATE 54   CHAÏM SOUTINE *Moïse Kisling, c.* 1925 (99 x 69 cm) Philadelphia, Museum of Art (Gift of Arthur Wiesenberger)

64

PLATE 55   CHAÏM SOUTINE *The Little Pastry Cook,* 1923 (72 x 44 cm) Paris, Louvre

PLATE 56   TSUGOUHARU FOUJITA *Youki, Goddess of the Snow*, 1924 (126 x 173 cm) Geneva, Musée Petit Palais

PLATE 57   Marc Chagall *Double Portrait of Bella and Marc Chagall*, 1924 (130 x 95 cm) Paris,
Katia Granoff Collection

PLATE 58   JULES PASCIN *Ginette and Mireille,* 1928 (93 x 73 cm) Paris, Musée du Petit Palais

PLATE 59   JULES PASCIN *The Blue Chemise*, 1929 (73 x 60 cm) Geneva, Musée Petit Palais

PLATE 60   JULES PASCIN *Nude with Red Sandals*, 1927 (65 x 54 cm) Geneva, Musée Petit Palais

THE ARTISTS

CONSTANTIN BRANCUSI

Born February 21, 1876, in Pestisani, Romania, of a family of poor farmers. At the age of nine he left his family, and through great hardship he earned his own living, learning by himself to read and write. He attended the School of Fine Arts in Bucharest, obtaining his diploma in 1902. Afterward he went to study in Munich, then set out on foot for Paris, where he arrived in 1904. He studied with the sculptor Antonin Mercier, but left him in 1906 to work by himself in a studio on boulevard du Montparnasse, which was frequented, after 1909, by the *Douanier* Henri Rousseau, Apollinaire, Max Jacob, and Modigliani. Having progressively abandoned naturalism after *The Kiss* (1908–10), he did *Maiastra,* from which must derive the successive versions of *Bird in Space* (1919–1940), his most famous work, together with *Mlle. Pogany* (1913–1933), *The Newborn* (1915), *Princess X* (1918), *The Cock* (1918), and the *Endless Column* carved from wood in 1918 and set up, in a steel version thirty-three meters high, at Tirgu Giu in Romania in 1937. Brancusi achieved international fame after his participation in the Armory Show in New York in 1913 and with his one-man show at the Brummer Gallery in New York. A large number of Brancusi's works are now in museums and private collections in the United States. However, he left as a legacy to the French nation all the works in his studio in ruelle Ronsin, where he first lived in 1918, at number eight, and in 1925, at number eleven, where he died March 16, 1957.

MARC CHAGALL

Born in 1887 in Vitebsk, Russia, of a middle-class Jewish family. His childhood was profoundly influenced by the ghetto environment and by the Hebrew religious rites, from which resulted the inspiration for all his work. After a brief period at the Imperial School of Fine Arts in St. Petersburg, he worked with Leon Bakst, the designer for the Ballet Russe, and went to Paris in 1910. He set up his studio in the artists' tenement called "the hive," exhibited at the Salon des Indépendents, and became acquainted with Blaise Cendrars, Apollinaire, Max Jacob, Robert Delaunay, and Modigliani. In 1914 he returned to Russia, stopping in Berlin, where he exhibited at the gallery of "The Storm." In 1915 he married Bella, who was the inspiration for many of his paintings of lovers, such as the *Double Portrait* of 1924. After the October Revolution of 1917, he was appointed Commissioner of Fine Arts in his native

city and also worked for the new Jewish Theater of Moscow. In 1922 he again left Russia for Berlin and returned to Paris in 1923. Ambroise Vollard immediately commissioned him to do a series of etchings for *Dead Souls* by Gogol and *The Fables* by La Fontaine, which were not published until thirty years later, as were his illustrations for the Bible. In the meantime he was developing a rich pictorial style that, after his attempt to reconcile the rigidness of Cubism with the violence of

MODIGLIANI *Portrait of the Poet Jean Cocteau,* 1917–18, Paris, Galerie Mouradian-Vallotton

Expressionism, found complete freedom in a more subjective inspiration and in an outpouring of color. After 1935 he returned to a more dramatic style to express the terror and sadness of the times. Having received the Carnegie prize in 1939, he found refuge in the United States in 1941, but in 1949 he returned to Paris, where the Museum of Modern Art gave him his first large retrospective show, later presented at the Stedelijk Museum in Amsterdam and at the Tate Gallery in London. Since that time Chagall has worked mainly on Biblical themes—paintings that are to be collected in a museum on the Côte d'Azur, where he has lived since 1950, and windows for the great cathedrals of Metz and Reims, and a set of twelve windows that decorate the synagogue of the Hadassah Hospital in Jerusalem.

ANDRÉ DERAIN

Born June 7, 1880, in Chatou on the Seine near Paris. After finishing grade school, he gave up further study to devote himself to painting. In 1899 he joined Vlaminck, who also lived in Chatou, and the two friends worked together in one studio. From this friendship sprang the most violent of the Fauve paintings. Encouraged in his work by the older Matisse, whom he had accompanied in the south, Derain sent his first Fauve paintings to the Salon d'Automne in 1905, where, together with those of Matisse, Vlaminck, and other painters who were attracted by pure color, they were collected in a central room that the critic Louis Vauxcelles called "the cage of wild beasts." In 1907, following a stay in London, Derain produced his series of *Bridges on the Thames* and *Hyde Park,* his finest Fauve paintings, as well as his sketches on the bank of the Seine in Chatou and Marly. But after 1908 the fires of Fauvism died down on the palettes of Derain and Vlaminck, both of whom had gone over to Cézanne. Under this influence Derain, who visited the "floating laundry" of Montmartre and there met Picasso and Braque, approved of Cubism without joining it, as his own taste was for more traditional styles of painting. He underwent a period of hieratic primitivism, possibly influenced by his discovery of Negro sculpture but more evidently Byzantine or Gothic in feeling. Finally, after 1920, in his landscapes, still lifes, figures, portraits, and compositions, Derain became fixed in a very traditional classicism. His creative spirit was annulled by his formal knowledge and his virtuosity as an imitator. After 1908 he stopped exhibiting at the salons and had only two one-man shows in France, in 1916 and in 1931, at Paul Guillaume's gallery. In 1935 he settled in Chambourcy, near Saint-Germain-en-Laye, where he lived in retirement until his death on September 8, 1954.

TSUGOHARU FOUJITA

Born November 27, 1886, in Kunamoto in the south of Japan, of a samurai family. His father was a doctor and a major in the Japanese army. After studying the techniques of both traditional Japanese and European painting at the School of Fine Arts in Tokyo from 1907 to 1912, the young artist left for Paris in 1913. He settled in Montparnasse, where, with his straight-cut bangs, his tortoise-shell glasses, his earrings, and his checked shirts,

MODIGLIANI *Portrait of Simon Mondzain,* 1917, Copenhagen, Private Collection

he became one of its most picturesque figures. In the twenties he achieved a reputation for his personal style, which combined the delicacy of Japanese drawing with Western naturalism. Shortly after his arrival, he took a studio in the Cité Falguiere, near Soutine and Modigliani. During the war, in 1917, he lived in rue Delambre with his first wife, a Frenchwoman, Fernande Barrey, and signed a contract with the dealer Chéron, who also handled Modigliani's work. A little later Zborowski took Foujita to Cagnes, together with his friends Soutine and Modigliani.

Foujita had begun to paint rather elaborate Parisian landscapes, but it is to his nudes (his second wife, Youki), to his portraits (that of the Countess Anna of Noailles), to his still lifes of familiar objects, and to his cats that he owes his fame and fortune. Like Van Dongen, he led the life of the successful artist in Paris, Deauville, and Cannes. During World War II, he returned to Japan but came back to Paris at the end of the war.

Foujita became a convert to Catholicism and was baptized in Reims in 1959 with the new name of Leonard, as he was a great admirer of Leonardo da Vinci. He died in Paris in 1969.

GABRIEL FOURNIER

Born in Grenoble, May 23, 1893. He attended the School of Fine Arts of Lyon and later, in 1912, the School of Decorative Arts in Paris. In 1914 he exhibited for the first time at the Salon des Indépendents and became a habitué of Montparnasse, where he met Kisling, Modigliani, Max Jacob, Cendrars, Louis Durey, and Erik Satie. In 1916, at La Rotonde, he met the poet and art dealer Léopold Zborowski, who later offered him a contract. Although he was interested in the experiments of his friends of Montparnasse, Gabriel Fournier found his own pictorial expression in traditional French art as it was carried on, after the Impressionists, by Bonnard and Dufy, whom Fournier helped when they were undertaking their new, decorative styles. Despite assiduous production in easel paintings and in large murals, Fournier rarely exhibited in public, and it was necessary to attend his posthumous retrospective show held in 1969 at the Hôtel de Sens in Paris to grasp the extent and the quality of his work. He died April 13, 1963, at his home in Fontainebleau, where he had lived since 1957.

PAUL GUILLAUME

Born in Paris in 1893, this art critic and dealer in French paintings was, with Apollinaire, one of the discoverers of Negro art. He shortly set himself up as a defender of the modern painters of his time, exhibiting to the public and to collectors, in his gallery in rue de la Boetie, the work of Modigliani and Soutine, as well as that of Matisse, Picasso, Derain, Utrillo, and the *Douanier* Rousseau.

Although Zborowski was the chief supporter of

Modigliani and Soutine, it was Paul Guillaume who did the most to promote them, especially Soutine, for whom, after 1923, he sold a large quantity of canvases to Dr. Albert Barnes, a wealthy American collector.

Paul Guillaume died in 1934, still a young man. He had assembled a very choice collection, which his widow, later the wife of Jean Walter, donated to the Louvre.

FOURNIER *Russians at the Rotonde*, 1917, Fontainebleau, Fournier Collection

MODIGLIANI *Portrait of Gabriel Fournier*, 1917, Fontainebleau, Fournier Collection

MAX JACOB

Born in Quimper, Brittany, in 1876. He was a French poet of Jewish origin.

In Montmartre and Montparnasse Max Jacob

Modigliani *Portrait of Paul Guillaume*, 1915, Paris, Private Collection

was a friend of all the avant-garde artists, but especially of the Cubists, whom he and Apollinaire ardently supported. Modigliani, who was one of his friends, made many portraits of him in 1916 and 1917.

He died in 1944 in the camp at Drancy, where the German occupation forces had interned him. He had been arrested at his retreat in Saint-Benoit-sur-Loire, near the abbey; he had been led there many years earlier by his conversion to the Christian faith.

MOISE KISLING

Son of a Jewish tailor, he was born in Krakow, Poland, January 22, 1891. Gifted with a great ability for drawing, he entered the Academy in Krakow at the age of fifteen. His professor, Pankiewicz, introduced him to the art of the Impressionists and urged him to pursue his studies in Paris, where Kisling went in 1910. He settled in Montparnasse, and his studio in rue Joseph Bara soon became a meeting place for artists and models

attracted there, night and day, by his genial generosity and assistance, which later benefited him in his career as a fashionable artist and portraitist of actresses and society women.

In the beginning, however, he had painted nostalgic figures of children and adolescents like those of Modigliani, who was his close friend and his companion in work as well as pleasure and whom he helped until his death. Wounded and removed from duty at the beginning of World War I, in which he fought in the Foreign Legion, Kisling became a naturalized citizen and settled in Paris, after a brief stay in Spain. In 1940 he went to America and remained there about six years. He returned to France in August, 1946. His style is characterized by brilliant color and forms, which are voluptuous but occasionally weak. He also did book illustrations. He died in 1953 on the Côte d'Azur, where he had done numerous paintings.

HENRI LAURENS

French sculptor, born February 18, 1885, in Paris. He began an apprenticeship in sculpture at the age of thirteen, and the method of carving directly into the stone strengthened his sense of form and prepared him, after his meeting with Georges Braque in 1911, to attempt the applica-

Modigliani *Portrait of the Poet Max Jacob*, 1915–16, Paris, Galerie Mouradian-Vallotton

76

tion of Cubist principles to sculpture. At that time he produced geometric still lifes and Cubist figures, most often in cut stone but also in terracotta and mixed materials. He also did a great number of remarkable papiers collés.

Laurens continued to work in the Cubist style until 1928, then progressively softened his style in his female figures in the round, to which he gave great luminosity and monumentality.

He had begun his career in Montmartre, but around 1915 he set up his studio in a summer house in Villa Brune, south of the fourteenth arrondissement, where he remained for the rest of his life. In this same year he met Modigliani and the latter painted portraits of Laurens.

He died May 5, 1954, in Paris.

JACQUES LIPCHITZ

Born August 22, 1891, at Druskieniki in Lithuania. He came to Paris in 1909 to study sculpture at the School of Fine Arts and in the free academies. After a brief return to Russia in 1912, he went back almost immediately to Paris, settling in the boulevard du Montparnasse.

After 1913 he became acquainted with Picasso, and in 1918 he met Max Jacob, Jean Cocteau, and Modigliani, but it was after his meeting with Juan Gris in 1916 that he went over to the Cubist style completely. Following its tenets, he painted still lifes in bas-relief and massive figures, and around 1926 he began to create, in forged or fused metal, sculptures characterized by an interplay of solids and voids. This new freedom of forms in space was his original contribution to Cubist sculpture. After completing several monumental and nearly abstract works, such as *The Song of Vowels* in 1931, Lipchitz evolved toward a more figurative expression of forms in baroque movement. He became a French citizen in 1925 and made his home in Boulogne-sur-Seine. In 1941 he settled in the United States, where he had a brilliant career, winning important commissions and prizes. After the end of World War II, retrospective shows of his work took place in many museums in America and Europe.

At present he resides in the United States, in Hastings-on-Hudson, New York, where he has built a studio; he makes regular visits to Italy, near Carrara, where he finds marble adapted to his sculpture.

AMEDEO MODIGLIANI

Born July 12, 1884, in Leghorn, the fourth son of Flaminio Modigliani and Eugenia Garcin. The Modigliani family, of Jewish origin, came from a village of the same name south of Rome. The grandfather, a banker in Rome, settled later in Leghorn, where his eldest son, Flaminio, had an insurance agency. The Garcin family was from Marseille. During the winter of 1895, young Amedeo, who was finishing his secondary studies at the Lyceum of Leghorn, had an attack of pleurisy. In 1899 he was ill with typhoid fever, followed by pulmonary complications, and in 1901 he had a relapse of tuberculosis, which tormented him all his life and was the cause of his early death. In 1902 he studied at the School of Fine Arts in Florence and in 1903 at the School of Fine Arts in Venice. Toward the end of 1905, Modigliani arrived in Paris and first lived in a small hotel in rue du Dôme near the Place de l'Étoile, then in a room in rue Caulaincourt, in the vicinity of the "floating laundry," where he soon met Picasso. He also met Utrillo in Montmartre. November of 1907 began his friendship with Dr. Alexandre, who soon became his supporter, and the buyer of his first paintings, and of whom he made three successive portraits. In 1908 Modigliani exhibited for the first time at the Salon des Indépendants. In 1909 he left the Right Bank and moved to Montparnasse, 14 Cité Falguiere, where he met the Romanian sculptor Brancusi, who occupied a

Modigliani *Portrait of Moïse Kisling*, 1915, Milan, Patani Collection

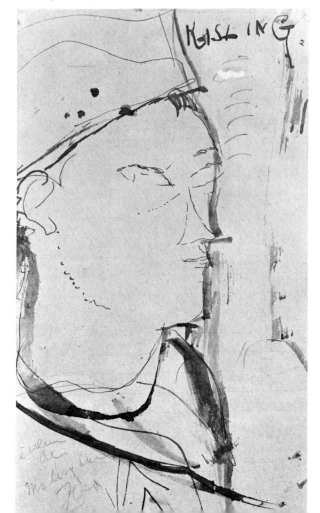

nearby studio. At that time Modigliani also wanted to become a sculptor. In the autumn he returned to Leghorn and very likely stopped at Carrara to obtain marble.

In 1912 he exhibited a group of seven sculptures

Modigliani *Portrait of Jeanne Hébuterne*, 1917–18, Paris, Private Collection

at the Salon d'Automne. In 1914 he was introduced to Beatrice Hastings, whom he lived with for several years, and to Léopold Zborowski, who was to become his dealer after 1916. In the meantime Paul Guillaume bought a few of his canvases, and Modigliani also worked for a brief time for Chéron, another art dealer from rue de la Boetie, who also aided Foujita. Modigliani, a frequent visitor of La Rotonde, was friendly with Soutine, Zadkine, Pascin, Ortiz de Zarate, and Kisling, in whose studio he worked. In 1917 he met Jeanne Hébuterne (born April 6, 1898). Also in 1917 Zborowski organized the first one-man show of Modigliani's paintings, from December 3 to December 30, in the Berthe Weill Gallery in rue Lafitte.

In April, 1918, Zborowski took Soutine, Foujita, and Modigliani to Cagnes. The latter prolonged his stay on the Côte d'Azur in Nice, in the home of the Survages, with Jeanne Hébuterne, who gave birth to a daughter, Jeanne, on November 29, 1918.

But Modigliani's health was deteriorating. He returned to Paris and took a studio on the top floor facing the courtyard, at 8 rue de la Grande Chaumiere. A year later, worn out by tuberculosis and by his disordered way of life, Modigliani had to be taken to Charity Hospital by his friends, where he died a few days later, on the night of January 25 or the early morning of January 26, 1920. At dawn the next day, Jeanne Hébuterne committed suicide by throwing herself from the window of her parents' apartment.

JULES PASCIN

Born Julius Pincas (of which Pascin is an anagram), March 3, 1885, in Widdin, Bulgaria, of a Spanish father and an Italian mother. He studied in Vienna and then in Munich, where he had, while still very young, great success as a satirical artist for the review, *Semplicissimus*. He went to Paris for the first time in 1905 and stayed there between his numerous journeys. In 1914, at the beginning of World War I, he settled in the United States, was naturalized in 1920, and returned to Paris in October, 1922.

From that time on, he led a luxurious and dissolute life surrounded by friends, male and female,

Modigliani *Portrait of Pablo Picasso*, 1915, Paris, Mme René Laporte Collection

and parasites. His dealers, the Bernheim brothers, sold his pictures easily and at high prices, particularly to American clients. His favorite subjects were women and girls, nude or seminude, modeled in iridescent halftones, frequently with a lascivious expression that betrays his disturbed

MODIGLIANI *Portrait of Diego Rivera,* 1914–15.
Paris, Musée National d'Art Moderne

his meetings with Modigliani, who made many pencil drawings and a portrait of Picasso in 1915, which is now in the collection of Georges Moos in Geneva. It would be ineffectual to attempt a complete biographical résumé of the celebrated Spanish artist.

DIEGO RIVERA

Mexican painter, born in 1886 in Guanajuato, Mexico. He lived in Paris from 1920 to 1921, was interested in the experiments of Picasso, Braque, and Juan Gris at the "floating laundry," but he visited more often the painters of Montparnasse. He made the acquaintance of Modigliani, who one day sketched his portrait (1914–15), which remained unfinished.

Rivera, carried away by his social and political ideas, diligently frequented La Rotonde, where the group of emigrant Russian revolutionaries, including Trotsky, constantly met. On his return to Mexico, he set himself up as a painter of the national revolution and developed a personal, monumental style, producing in 1922 the modern Mexican mural in the amphitheater of the University of Mexico City. This mural was followed by many other official commissions. With Rivera in this new Mexican mural school are Orozco and Siqueiros.

He died in Mexico City in 1957.

CHAÏM SOUTINE

Son of a poor clothes mender, he was born in 1894 in the small Jewish community of the village of Smilovitchi, Lithuania. To escape from ghetto poverty and religious restraints, young Chaïm, barely thirteen, fled to Minsk, then to Vilna, where he entered the School of Fine Arts, attended also by Kikoine and Kremegne, whom he met again later in Paris. In 1911, with the help of a doctor who had taken an interest in him and at the instigation of Kremegne, he set out for Paris. He rejoined Kremegne in the community of artists called "the hive," where, for a time, he occupied one of the cells. Later he settled in the rue Saint Gothard and still later, when assured of success, in a modern studio of Villa Seurat in the neighborhood of Parc Montsouris. In Montparnasse he soon met Modigliani, who became his only intimate friend, except for his two compatriots from Vilna. The portraits that Modigliani and Soutine made of each other are testimony to their friendship. In 1918 Modigliani introduced Soutine to Zborowski, and the latter launched him toward success with the help of Paul Guillaume and Dr.

mentality and dissolute life. In spite of his continuous success, he took his own life on June 2, 1930, on the day of the opening of his show at the Georges Petit Gallery. He hung himself and was found by his friend and compatriot, Papazoff, in his studio at 30 boulevard de Clichy, in Montmartre.

PABLO PICASSO

Born October 25, 1881, in Málaga (Andalusia), son of José Ruiz and Maria Picasso. After making three trips to Paris, he returned there in April, 1904, and settled definitively, at first in rue Ravignan in a studio of the famous "floating laundry," where Cubism was born and where he remained until 1909, and then in boulevard de Clichy. In 1912 Picasso abandoned Montmartre for the Left Bank and settled at 242 boulevard Raspail, and the following year at 5 rue Schoeler. But Picasso did not care for Montparnasse, nor for the Bohemian life of its inhabitants, and in 1918, after the war, he took an apartment in rue de la Boetie.

These few facts must suffice as a framework for

Albert Barnes, who, in 1923, bought every canvas in his studio. In the meantime Zborowski sent Soutine to Céret to work, then to Cagnes. There he painted most of his landscapes, distorted like his early still lifes and figures. The innate unrest and frenetic inspiration of Soutine are revealed in all his paintings, which are done in heavy impasto and burning color, as in such masterpieces as *The Little Pastry Cook* (1922–23) or the famous series of ox carcasses (1925). At the outbreak of World War II, Soutine took refuge in Touraine, at Chamignu-sur-Veude, but in 1943 an intestinal perforation necessitated his transferal to a Paris hospital, where he died on August 9, 1943.

LÉOPOLD SURVAGE

Born July 31, 1879, in Moscow, of a Finnish father and Danish mother. He attended the School of Fine Arts after his precocious talent as a pianist gave way to that of painter. Attracted by the work of the French artists, Cézanne, Gauguin, and especially Matisse, which he saw in the Tchoukine Collection, he decided to go to Paris, where he arrived in July, 1908. There he developed a personal style bordering on Cubism, with whose

MODIGLIANI *Portrait of Chaïm Soutine*, 1917, Paris, Private Collection

followers he exhibited at the Salon des Indépendents in 1911. The following year, experimenting further, he created abstract rhythms of colored forms. Later his work became more poetic but still subjected to a kind of Cubist discipline. Among his friends were Delaunay, Severini, Brancusi, and Modigliani. In 1918, at the request of Zborowski, he took the ailing Modigliani to Cagnes, and later he and his wife welcomed Modigliani to their home in Nice.

Survage became a naturalized French citizen in 1927. In 1969, shortly before his death at the age of ninety, he was given a retrospective exhibit at the Galliéra Museum in Paris.

KEES VAN DONGEN

Cornelius Theodorus Marie (called Kees) van Dongen was born January 27, 1877, in Delfshaven, a suburb of Rotterdam, where his father was the head of a malt factory. There he did his apprenticeship, but he showed a precocious talent for drawing and soon began study at the Academy of Fine Arts in Rotterdam. After an early visit to Paris in 1897, he finally settled there in 1899, in Montmartre. Around 1905 he had a studio in the "floating laundry." In 1904 he met André Derain and Maurice Vlaminck and quickly became an adherent of Fauvism, to which he long remained attached because of his sensuous temperament, though as a stylish portraitist he had occasionally to tone down his spirit to satisfy his society and demimonde clientele. By 1912 he was established, and in 1917, when he moved to Villa Said in the elegant district of Auteuil, he was quite well known. Earlier he lived in rue Denfert-Rochereau and led a gay life in Montparnasse, vying more with Foujita than with his earlier friends at the Salon d'Automne of 1905. Nevertheless, his qualities as a fine artist were confirmed by the retrospective show that the Museum of Modern Art in Paris gave him in 1967 to celebrate his ninetieth birthday. He died a short while later, May 28, 1968, in Monaco, where he had lived for his last ten years.

MAURICE VLAMINCK

Born in Paris, in the district of Les Halles, April 4, 1876. His father, of Flemish extraction, was a violinist, and his mother, from Lorraine, was a piano teacher. After his parents moved to Vesinet, on the banks of the Seine, Vlaminck earned his living playing the violin in dance orchestras in the area when he was not taking part in bicycle races. His first marriage was to Suzanne Berly in 1894.

He soon met Derain in Chatou, and the two formed the School of Chatou that was the beginning of Fauvism. In 1902 he published *From One Bed to Another*, a novel illustrated by André Derain. After 1906 Vlaminck was a frequenter of the "floating laundry" and Picasso's group, and he soon renounced the violence of Fauvism for the influence, although only superficially, of Cézanne. From 1908 to 1917 he painted many landscapes and still lifes in a style of brushwork that recalls Cézanne's. Later, following the example of Derain but without the latter's intellectual preoccupations, his style became academic, a concise, romantic realism in monotones with black as a dominant color. After 1918 he retired to the country, first in Valmondois, then in Rueil-la-Gadeliere in the department of Eure-et-Loir. There in 1925 he acquired a large farm, La Tourilliere, where he lived with his wife and their five daughters. His several exhibits and the ten canvases shown at the Venice Biennale in 1954 were well received and testified again to his international success as a painter. He died at his farm, La Tourilliere, in 1958.

OSSIP ZADKINE

Son of a professor of classical languages and of a Scottish mother, Zadkine was born in Smolensk, Russia, July 14, 1890. After completing studies at the Polytechnic School of Arts and Crafts in London, he went to Paris in 1909, full of enthusiasm, illusions, and hope, and spent several months at the School of Fine Arts, in Inglebert's class. Later he left it and settled in "the hive" to work independently. There and in Montparnasse he made the acquaintance of other independent artists, such as Chagall, Soutine, Léger, Picasso, Brancusi, Delaunay, the poet Max Jacob, Apollinaire, Salmon, Cendrars, and Modigliani, who at that time was still working in sculpture. It was Zad-

During his early years in Paris, his first experiments were influenced by Negro sculpture and Cubism, with which he had become acquainted at the same time.

His activity was interrupted by the outbreak of World War I, in which he fought as a volunteer until he was invalided out in 1917 after being overcome by gas. Afterward, year by year, his personal style was affirmed in a new plastic expression based on the opposition of convex and concave forms rhythmically but firmly organized and always highly expressive. When he died in 1969, Ossip Zadkine had occupied for many years a very important place in the history of contemporary world sculpture.

Derain *Portrait of Maurice Vlaminck*, 1903

LÉOPOLD ZBOROWSKI

Of Polish origin, he came to Paris to study literature at the Sorbonne, but he soon became an art dealer. With his wife, Anna, he lived in a building of studios at 3 rue Joseph Bara, near Kisling's house. Meeting with artists of Montparnasse at the cafes of Le Dôme and La Rotonde, he began dealing with artists as much to help them to eat and to paint as to earn his own living. He was most interested in Soutine and Modigliani, whom Soutine had introduced to Zborowski. He succeeded in launching Soutine by means of Paul Guillaume's sales to the wealthy Dr. Barnes, but he had less success with Modigliani, whom he nevertheless helped all his life. Zborowski was very extravagant and went through high and low points in his career as a dealer. In 1927 he opened his own gallery at the corner of rue de Seine and rue Visconti. But he squandered the considerable funds that he made and died a poor man, after a year's illness, March 24, 1932, perhaps not yet fifty. The date of his birth is not known.

List of Illustrations

Translated by Helen I. Hubbard

PLATE 52   Moïse Kisling *Kiki of Montparnasse with Red Sweater and Blue Kerchief,* 1925 (92 x 65 cm)
Geneva, Musée Petit Palais

PLATE 51   MOÏSE KISLING *Nude on a Red Couch*, 1918 (60 x 73 cm) Geneva, Musée Petit Palais

PLATE 50   Moïse Kisling *Jean Cocteau in His Studio,* 1916 (73 x 60 cm) Geneva, Musée Petit Palais

60

PLATE 49   ANDRÉ DERAIN *Léopold Zborowski*, 1922 (44 x 37 cm) Milan, Private Collection